American Moments

ABDO
& Daughters

THE INDUSTRIAL REVOLUTION

By Alan Pierce

Published by ABDO Publishing Company, 4940 Viking Drive, Suite 622, Edina, Minnesota 55435. Copyright © 2005 by Abdo Consulting Group, Inc. International copyrights reserved in all countries. No part of this book may be reproduced in any form without written permission from the publisher. ABDO & Daughters™ is a trademark and logo of ABDO Publishing Company.

Printed in the United States.

Edited by: Melanie A. Howard
Interior Production and Design: Terry Dunham Incorporated
Cover Design: Mighty Media
Photos: Corbis, Library of Congress

Library of Congress Cataloging-in-Publication Data

Pierce, Alan, 1966-
   The Industrial Revolution / Alan Pierce.
      p. cm. -- (American moments)
   Includes index.
   ISBN 1-59197-933-1
   1. Industrial revolution--United States--Juvenile literature. 2. Industrial revolution--Great Britain--Juvenile literature. I. Title. II. Series.

HC105.P39 2005
330.973'05--dc22

                                                    2004055421

CONTENTS

REVOLUTION

In the nineteenth century, many American children did not attend school. They were too busy working long hours in factories and mines. These children toiled around machinery that often maimed them. Boys labored in coal mines where they sometimes became sick with black lung disease. These hardships were not rare. In 1820, half of the country's industrial workers were children.

Child labor was not new. Children had always worked on farms and performed tasks for their families. But working in dangerous factories was a new development for children. This was because factories were a recent phenomenon in the nineteenth century. Before that time, most manufacturing took place in small shops and homes.

The growth of factories was part of an event known as the Industrial Revolution. During the Industrial Revolution, machines and other technologies such as steam power replaced the muscles of humans and animals. The Industrial Revolution also gave rise to new modes of transportation such as steamboats and trains. These inventions made travel easier and faster.

The word *revolution* is normally used to describe political changes such as the overthrow of a government. The Industrial Revolution was not this kind of event. Instead, the Industrial Revolution is called a revolution because of its sweeping impact on society.

Young boys work at a textile mill in Hickory, North Carolina.

Women, children, and men left the home to work in factories. More people left farms to work in cities. The Industrial Revolution transformed the United States from an agricultural nation to a manufacturing giant.

FARMS AND FACTORIES

The United States became a manufacturing force, but the Industrial Revolution did not begin there. Instead, it arose in Britain in the eighteenth century. Britain possessed many qualities that made the Industrial Revolution possible. Coal and water were both necessary to power the new machines that would increase production. Britain had coal mines, rivers, and harbors. In addition, the nation had established a strong financial system. This meant that money was available to invest in new inventions and factories.

Britain had also experienced major changes in farming that prepared the way for the Industrial Revolution. For centuries, British farmers had raised crops on land they shared with other farmers. After the harvest, livestock was allowed to graze on the fields. A policy called enclosure altered this system. Enclosure started as early as the twelfth century, but the process accelerated in the eighteenth century. Under enclosure, fields were fenced off or separated by hedges.

Enclosure had a dramatic effect on British agriculture. Because farmers now controlled their own land, they became more willing to experiment with crop production. Farmers improved the use of fertilizers and began to use crop rotation. A British farmer named Jethro Tull invented a horse-drawn seed drill. This drill allowed

Pictured below are two seed drills. The one on the right was made in the mid-nineteenth century. The newer seed drill on the left was designed to be pulled, rather than pushed.

farmers to plant crops in rows. This method of planting made it easier for farmers to clear weeds. These changes in farming are sometimes called the agricultural revolution. This revolution increased food production and lowered the cost of food in Britain.

But enclosure also hurt many farmers. Families were sometimes unable to support themselves on small plots of enclosed land. Also, many farmers had depended on the open, common land to graze their livestock. The loss of this land meant they could no longer raise cattle and hogs. Many were forced to give up farming. Consequently, many people were available to work in other areas.

There is another reason the Industrial Revolution occurred in Britain. The country was a colonial power. In the eighteenth century, Britain and France fought for dominance of India in the Seven Years' War. When the war ended in 1763, Britain had established control of India. The Indian colonies provided Britain with an abundance of cotton. Clothing made from cotton was popular. This fabric was more comfortable than wool and was easier to wash.

Throughout much of the eighteenth century, Britain relied on the putting-out system to make textiles. This method called for merchants to drop off wool or cotton at individual homes. Residents then spun the material into thread or weaved thread into cloth. The merchants paid the spinners or weavers when the material was finished. However, as Britain's population grew, the putting-out method could no longer supply enough cloth.

Weavers benefited from the mechanical talent of John Kay. As the son of a woolen manufacturer, Kay was skilled with textile equipment. In 1733, he secured a patent for an invention called the flying shuttle. The shuttle is a device on a loom that runs thread horizontally between other threads. Two weavers were needed to operate an old-style shuttle. The new flying shuttle allowed one weaver to run the loom and produce more fabric than two weavers.

The success of the flying shuttle, however, created a problem for textile producers. Weavers became more efficient, but workers who made thread and yarn were unable to keep up with demand. The Royal Society for the encouragement of Arts, Manufactures and

Commerce even offered money for the invention of a machine that could spin more thread.

In 1754, James Hargreaves began working on an improved spinning machine. By 1768, he had a successful invention called the spinning jenny, which was named after his wife. The spinning jenny was an improvement because workers no longer needed to draw cotton fibers out by hand. Instead, the machine drew out the fibers. Also, the spinning jenny spun eight threads at the same time. Eventually, Hargreaves sold some of these new machines to textile mills.

A spinning jenny

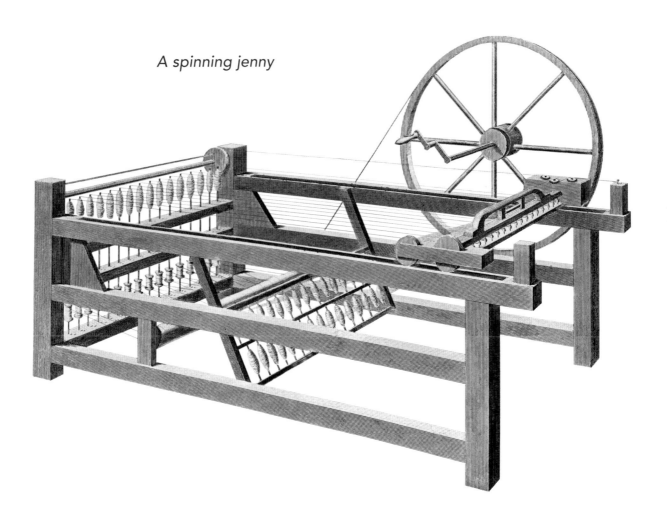

Local people feared Hargreaves's invention. They realized they could lose their jobs to the machine. In 1768, they attacked Hargreaves's home and destroyed his spinning jenny. Hargreaves and his family moved to another part of Britain.

The flying shuttle and spinning jenny vastly increased textile production. But these machines were still powered by hand. In 1769, Sir Richard Arkwright worked on the idea for another spinning machine. Arkwright used rollers to draw apart the fibers. This made cotton thread less coarse. At first, the rollers were powered by horses walking on treadmills. Arkwright then invented the water frame to use waterpower to drive the rollers.

Sir Richard Arkwright

Arkwright's water frame had a major impact on the spinning process. The water frame made it necessary for spinning to take place in buildings located near rivers or streams. Workers could no longer stay at home to make thread. They had to leave their homes to work at the mills. This was the beginning of the factory method of production. Some workers did not accept this change gladly. In one case, workers attacked one of Arkwright's mills.

LUDDITES

The technology of the Industrial Revolution provoked resentment among some people. In the eighteenth century, some workers destroyed textile machinery. But one of the more famous examples of protest against technology occurred in the early nineteenth century. A group of workers known as Luddites demolished textile machinery in Britain.

Fearful neighbors destroy Hargreaves's spinning jenny.

The Luddites were textile workers who claimed to follow a probably imaginary leader named King Ludd or Ned Ludd. They were angry because a new machine used to make stockings hurt their livelihood. Because of this machine, workers received less pay or even lost their jobs. The Luddites wanted craftsmanship appreciated and machines eliminated. Wearing masks, the Luddites entered homes at night to destroy textile machinery.

The Luddites carried out most of their destruction in 1811–1812. After the violence increased, the British government took steps to subdue the Luddites. The government's efforts led to several Luddites being charged with crimes and hanged. By 1813, the Luddites had ceased most of their attacks, although a few incidents occurred later.

The word Luddite is still used today. But it now refers to a person who is against technological change.

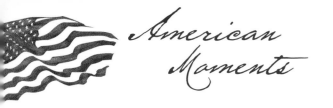

STEAM POWER

Waterpower did not remain the dominant form of energy in the Industrial Revolution. Steam eventually provided the most important source of energy. Europeans had long known that steam could be used as an energy source. Two English engineers named Thomas Newcomen and Thomas Savery developed a piston-operated steam pump in 1712. Improvements were made to Newcomen's engine, but steam engines still wasted most of their energy.

In the winter of 1763, a Scott named James Watt began his work on steam engines. He was asked to repair a model of Newcomen's engine at the University of Glasgow in Scotland. Watt realized that the engine's design caused the machine to waste most of its energy. He developed some improvements that greatly improved the steam engine. For example, he designed a separate condenser that allowed the engine's cylinder to remain hot. This kept the engine from losing much of its heat.

Watt began work as a surveyor for canal construction in Scotland in 1766. This undertaking prevented him from devoting his full attention to steam engines. However, he prepared a patent for his invention, which he received in 1769. In the next decade, Watt received financial support that allowed him to concentrate on making the steam engine better. At this time, Watt's engines were beginning to be used at coal mines and ironworks.

JAMES WATT

The Industrial Revolution probably could not have happened without James Watt's improvements to the steam engine. Watt gained much of his mechanical experience as a boy in his father's shop. His father was a shipbuilder and provided Watt with his own set of tools. With these, Watt made models of ship parts he saw in the shop. He was later apprenticed to a mathematical instrument maker in London, England. Afterward, he returned to Scotland and became a maker of scientific instruments for the University of Glasgow.

James Watt

Watt was first introduced to Newcomen's steam engine at the university. After improving the engine, he began a thriving business creating and improving steam engines. He later formed a partnership with manufacturer and engineer Matthew Boulton. By 1800, there were 500 Boulton and Watt engines in use around the world. However, Watt's patents expired that year. Other inventors rushed to create new and better steam engines. Watt decided to retire, though he continued inventing.

By the time he died in 1819, Watt had invented the press-copier, which is like today's photocopiers. He had also developed the measurement called horsepower. We now use his name, Watt, as a term for a measurement of electrical power. His inventions continue to be used in manufacturing to this day.

In 1781, Watt developed the sun-and-planet gear. This device allowed the steam engine to produce a rotary motion that could power machinery. The steam engine could then be used to run machines in ironworks and textile mills.

TECHNOLOGY SPREADS

Britain attempted to keep its technology a secret from other countries. Exporting machines was illegal. Britons were not even allowed to describe industrial machinery to foreigners. In addition, mechanics were forbidden to leave the country.

These measures failed to prevent the spread of knowledge about technology. Samuel Slater had worked as an apprentice in a British textile mill since about 1783. During his apprenticeship, he became supervisor of machinery and mill construction. However, he believed that the United States offered better prospects in the textile industry. Efforts to copy British technology in the United States had failed. But the United States offered rewards for workers who were experts in cotton manufacturing.

In 1789, Slater boarded a ship for the United States. One popular story says that Slater left disguised as a farm laborer to avoid detection. Taking drawings of textile mills and machinery out of the country was

Samuel Slater

Samuel Slater's mill in Pawtucket, Rhode Island

illegal. So, Slater memorized the details of his textile plant. Later in the year, he arrived in New York where he worked briefly at a factory.

Slater soon received an offer from the Almy and Brown textile company in Rhode Island. He agreed to build machinery based on British technology for a cotton mill. By December 1790, a mill using the new technology was in operation. Local children were trained to operate the machinery. Child labor had not been unusual in Slater's Britain where children worked in industry and mining.

Problems hindered the mill. Sufficiently clean raw cotton was hard to get. Machinery breakdowns were common. The company had a difficult time providing enough cotton yarn to meet demand. In 1793, the company built a mill on the Blackstone River near Pawtucket, Rhode Island. This mill was known as the Old Slater Mill. It was the first successful cotton mill in the United States.

Meanwhile, a new invention benefited the cotton industry. In 1793, Eli Whitney introduced a superior version of the cotton gin. This device mechanically removed seeds from cotton fibers. In the southern United States, slaves were used to raise and harvest cotton. A slave could remove seeds from one pound (.5 kg) of cotton in a day by hand. Whitney's cotton gin cleaned 50 pounds (23 kg) of cotton in one day.

Cotton became profitable to grow in the United States. Moreover, the demand at British and U.S. textile mills created a huge market for cotton. U.S. cotton exports grew from 500,000 pounds (227,000 kg) in 1793 to 18 million pounds (8,000,000 kg) in 1800.

The Industrial Revolution was not limited to Britain and the United States. An Englishman named William Cockerill introduced textile machinery to France in 1799. In modern-day Belgium, he set up wool-spinning machines. Eventually, huge textile factories sprang up in Liège in what is now eastern Belgium. The Industrial Revolution had arrived in continental Europe.

Political turmoil, however, prevented much of Europe from quickly imitating Britain's industrial success. France was ruled by Emperor Napoléon Bonaparte, who engaged in wars throughout Europe. For the most part, these wars delayed industrialization. Also, Germany was not a unified country at this time. It was divided into dozens of smaller states. This political division hurt commerce in this region in the early decades of the nineteenth century.

16

ELI WHITNEY

Eli Whitney is best known for inventing the cotton gin. However, this was not his greatest invention. Because his cotton gin failed to make a profit, Whitney became dedicated to producing firearms. On June 14, 1798, Whitney signed a contract with the U.S. government to make 4,000 guns by September 1799. The military's largest arms providers had only been able to produce 1,000 guns in the previous three years.

Nevertheless, Whitney was given $5,000 to begin his project. Muskets at that time were made by hand. Every piece of every

Eli Whitney

gun was different, which meant that parts for one musket might or might not fit in another musket. Whitney came up with the idea of standardized parts. His idea was to use machines to manufacture musket parts. This method would allow corresponding parts to be the same size and shape. Consequently, each part could be used interchangeably with any gun that Whitney produced.

Although Whitney did not meet his deadline, he did end up profiting from his new business. Whitney's notion of using standardized parts in guns has also been applied to many other items since 1798. Toys, cars, computers, and many other objects are made out of standardized parts. Whitney created what is known as the American mass-production system, which has flourished to this day.

FULTON'S FOLLY

In the United States, industry was forging ahead. One sign of this was the emergence of the steamboat. By 1787, an American silversmith named John Fitch had developed a boat powered by a steam engine. But this boat traveled too slowly upstream to be considered a success.

Another American named Robert Fulton was also interested in watercraft. He had developed a submarine in France for Napoléon. In 1800, Fulton tested the submarine, named the *Nautilus*. But the *Nautilus* was too slow to catch and sink sailing ships. The French lost interest in Fulton's submarine. Fulton presented his idea for a submarine to the British, but they turned down his concept. He then began to work on a steamboat.

Fulton's steamboat project received the support of Robert R. Livingston, the U.S. ambassador to France. Livingston also owned a monopoly for steamboat navigation in the state of New York. The two men formed a partnership, and Fulton began testing in France. Fulton's steamboat traveled at 3 mph (4.8 km/h). However, Livingston's monopoly depended on building steamboats that traveled at least 4 mph (6.4 km/h). In 1806, Fulton sailed to New York to improve his design.

By 1807, Fulton was ready to test his steamboat on the Hudson River. Some people scoffed at the boat and called it "Fulton's Folly."

Robert Fulton   Robert R. Livingston

Its actual name was the *Clermont*. In August, the *Clermont* sailed from New York City to Albany, New York. The boat made the 150-mile (241-km) journey upstream in about 32 hours. A sailboat usually took four days to cover the same route. Fulton had proven the superiority of his steamboat.

During the next few years, steamboat traffic spread to the Mississippi River. Fulton and Livingston began running a steamboat service from New Orleans, Louisiana, to Natchez in the Mississippi Territory. A riverboat captain named Henry Miller Shreve soon recognized that a different kind of steamboat was needed for the Mississippi River. The channels of the Mississippi were shallower than the Hudson River bed.

Early steamboats had problems that made them failures. As a result, some people doubted that Robert Fulton's steamboat the *Clermont* would be a success. However, the *Clermont* proved disbelievers wrong by traveling almost 5 mph (8 km/h) up the Hudson River. The *Clermont* was 133 feet (41 m) long and 18 feet (5 m) wide. Moreover, James Watt's company, Boulton and Watt, provided the steam engine for the *Clermont*. The *Clermont*'s run proved the steamboat was a reliable form of transportation. Passengers soon used steamboats to travel on the Hudson River.

In 1816, he introduced the steamboat *Washington*. This steamboat had a more powerful steam engine to push the boat against currents. It also had a shallower hull, or body. Shreve's design became the basis of later steamboat designs.

Steamboat traffic grew dramatically. In 1820, about 60 steamboats paddled along the Mississippi River. By 1860, the number of steamboats rose to about 1,000. These boats carried cotton, sugar, and people along the river.

Fulton also played a role in another development of the Industrial Revolution. In 1812, he served on a commission that favored building a canal. This canal would extend from Lake Erie to the Hudson River in New York. Some believed such a canal was needed to strengthen the state's commercial development. Settlers in western Pennsylvania and farther west shipped their products down the Ohio and Mississippi rivers. This was easier and cheaper than hauling these goods overland to the East Coast. Many in New York wanted access to this trade that was flowing to New Orleans.

New York governor DeWitt Clinton soon threw his support behind the Erie Canal project. But many people ridiculed the project and called it "Clinton's Big Ditch." Building the canal was an ambitious undertaking. The project called for digging a 363-mile (584-km) canal in New York from Buffalo to Albany. New York City would then be connected to western trade by the Hudson River. The state of New York provided $7 million to fund construction, which lasted from 1817 to 1825.

The Erie Canal turned out to be a tremendous success. Shipping costs dropped, and the time to transport goods from Buffalo to New York City fell sharply. These factors helped New York City continue

Several boats participate in celebrating the completion of the Erie Canal.

to be the country's greatest commercial center. Moreover, the canal provided a route for settlers to travel west to Michigan, Ohio, Indiana, and Illinois.

Other states wanted to reproduce New York's success. Pennsylvania, Ohio, and Indiana started massive canal projects in the 1820s and 1830s. The number of canal miles grew enormously. In 1810, there had been 100 miles (161 km) of canals in the United States. By 1840, the number had climbed to more than 3,300 miles (5,300 km). But the popularity of canal building eventually faded. A new method of transportation known as the railroad began to cross the American landscape.

RAILROAD REVOLUTION

The railroad, like many inventions of the Industrial Revolution, started in Britain. British miners had long used carts on wooden rails to haul coal from mines. People and animals pulled these carts. The arrival of the steam engine prompted some people to think about using this energy source to pull trams.

By 1803, English engineer Richard Trevithick had built a steam locomotive. He demonstrated his invention in London, England. Trevithick also built a steam railway for an ironworks in Wales. However, the cast-iron rails were unable to support Trevithick's engines.

Another mechanic named George Stephenson improved earlier locomotive designs. He worked at the Killingworth colliery in northeastern England. In 1814, Stephenson built a locomotive for the mine. The locomotive was named the Blücher, after Prussian general Gebhard Leberecht von Blücher. The engine was able to pull 30 tons (27 t) of coal at 4 mph (6.4 km/h). But the locomotive was expensive to run.

George Stephenson

One of George Stephenson's early steam locomotives

Stephenson continued to work on designs for his coal mine locomotives. In 1821, he learned about a plan to build an 8-mile (13-km) railway from Stockton to Darlington. The original plan called for using horses to pull carts along the line. But Stephenson insisted that a locomotive could pull 50 times more weight than the loads pulled by horses. After presenting his arguments, Stephenson was allowed to try his steam locomotive on the rail line.

The railway opened on September 27, 1825. A man on a horse rode along the track. Stephenson then started up the locomotive, which proceeded to pull wagons of 450 passengers at 15 mph (24 km). The message of the opening ceremony was clear. For transportation and hauling, the muscle of horses was giving way to the power of the steam locomotive.

Americans were excited about the new railroad technology. In 1827, business leaders in Baltimore, Maryland, planned a railway. It would stretch from their city to Wheeling in present-day West Virginia. They hoped this rail line would allow Baltimore to tap into western trade.

The United States, however, had no locomotives. This changed when the Delaware and Hudson Canal Company acquired locomotives from Britain. One of these locomotives was known as the Stourbridge Lion. On August 8, 1829, the Stourbridge Lion made a short test run near Honesdale, Pennsylvania. The Stourbridge Lion was the first locomotive to run on an American railway. In about a year, Americans began building their own locomotives.

In the 1830s, the railroad developed rapidly in the United States. The Baltimore & Ohio Railroad tested its first locomotive in 1830. At that time, hardly any railroad track existed in the country. By 1840, about 2,800 miles (4,500 km) of track crossed parts of the United States.

Railroad construction continued at an impressive pace. In 1860, the United States had 30,000 miles (48,280 km) of track. This was more railroad line than existed in the rest of the world combined.

Railroads greatly speeded up travel in the United States. In 1800, a week was needed to travel from New York City to Pittsburgh, Pennsylvania. By 1860, railroads had shortened this trip to less than a day.

Workers celebrate the completion of the transcontinental railroad.
This famous railway connected the eastern and western United States.

The growth of the railroad had other effects on the country.
Railroads, like canals, drove down shipping costs. But unlike canals,
railroads did not freeze over in winter. Trains could operate in all
kinds of weather.

Farmers who lived near railways benefited from cheaper shipping
costs. They generally received more money for their crops. Also,
their land was worth more. These more prosperous farmers had more
money to spend on manufactured goods, which spurred U.S. industry.

GROWING PAINS

As the railroad expanded in the United States, another sign of the Industrial Revolution began to spring up. More factories appeared in parts of the country. The textile industry had introduced factories to the United States. And this industry continued to build more factories, especially in the northeastern part of the country. This area of the country had plenty of streams and rivers to power machines in the textile factories.

Many factories employed children and women because they worked for cheaper wages. However, factory work remained somewhat rare for women. But hundreds of thousands of children worked in factories. By 1900, the number of children working in factories was about 1.7 million. Children often worked long hours in the factories. In some cotton mills, water was splashed on children's faces to keep them awake to work at night. Fatigue led to many deaths and accidents at work.

Long work days for young people were normal even near the beginning of the American Industrial Revolution. In the early decades of the nineteenth century, farm girls worked at the textile mills in Lowell, Massachusetts. One girl wrote in a letter that she worked 13 hours a day, not counting breaks for meals. When these girls were not working, they stayed at boardinghouses. Older women supervised the girls to make sure they behaved properly.

The Lowell National Historic Park was created in 1978 to preserve the history of the Lowell mills. Pictured here is the Boott Cotton Mills Museum. It is located on the east side of the park.

Conditions at the Lowell factories worsened in the 1840s. In order to compete with other textile manufacturers, the girls had to work longer hours for lower wages. One worker named Sarah G. Bagley opposed this treatment. In 1844, she established the Lowell Female Labor Reform Association. The association wanted better working conditions and a 10-hour workday. Bagley appealed to the Massachusetts legislature to become involved with these issues, but the government refused.

At this time, American workers became more organized to fight for better pay and shorter working hours. Labor unions began to appear as early as the 1820s. In the 1830s and 1840s, labor strikes became more common.

Employers sometimes used immigrants to take the place of striking workers. Immigrants were also hired because employers believed immigrant workers were easier to control. For example, in Lowell, immigrants began replacing American girls in the textile factories.

Europeans had immigrated to the United States throughout the nation's history. But the rate of immigration increased significantly in the 1840s. Ireland suffered a disastrous famine in the middle of the decade. This crisis forced many Irish people to emigrate to the United States. Also, the population of Europe was increasing. Many people chose to leave Europe, which seemed to be getting crowded. They ventured to the United States because that nation offered religious freedom and economic opportunity.

The wave of immigration contributed greatly to the industry and settlement of the United States. Irish workers helped build canals and railroads. Meanwhile, Germans farmed and set up towns in the upper Midwest.

An Irish family prepares to emigrate to the United States.

Immigration and industrialization transformed the United States. The population of the country was 5.3 million people in 1800. By 1860, the nation had 31.4 million people. Fewer Americans relied on farming for a living and more people lived in towns and cities. In 1820, there were 12 U.S. cities with more than 5,000 people. Thirty years later, 150 cities had grown to this size. More people still lived in rural areas. The country, however, was clearly becoming a place where people were leaving the farm for the city.

American Moments

WAR AND IMMIGRATION

In 1861, the Civil War broke out. This conflict erupted when 11 Southern states seceded from the United States. Slavery had contributed to the crisis. The South relied on slaves to work in cotton fields and to perform other tasks. Northern states had abolished slavery and many people there despised it.

Northern and Southern states also had different economic interests. Northern leaders favored tariffs, or taxes, on imported goods. These tariffs made foreign goods more expensive and protected the price of Northern manufactured goods. Southerners hated tariffs because these taxes forced them to pay more for manufactured products.

At the beginning of the war, the North had a far greater advantage in industrial capacity. More than 100,000 factories existed in the North. The South had about 18,000. Almost all of the nation's firearms and railroad equipment were made in the North. In addition, the North had most of the country's railroad tracks. These resources helped the North achieve victory in 1865.

Historians disagree about what kind of impact the war had on the country's industrialization. Manufacturing certainly grew during the war. Northern manufacturers produced more guns. Also, the number of factories doubled in the North between 1860 and 1870. On the

THE · NEW · SOUTH.

SUPPLEMENT TO HARPER'S WEEKLY, JANUARY 15, 1887.

Tredegar Iron Works was the Confederacy's major manufacturer of cannons during the U.S. Civil War.

other hand, some historians believe the war hurt industrialization. The war pulled hundreds of thousands of men from the workforce. Instead of producing goods, these men served in the military.

After the war, American industry continued to thrive. The country had the resources to support expanding industries. Coal, iron, and oil existed in abundance. Moreover, millions of immigrants continued to pour into the country. These new immigrants arrived from Italy, Austria-Hungary, Poland, and Russia. They provided more labor for the growing U.S. industries.

In addition, a new wave of immigrants came to the United States seeking religious freedom. This group included many Jewish immigrants, who were a minority in Europe. Also, many immigrants could earn more money than they could in their homelands.

The new immigrants settled in major American cities. But U.S. cities were undergoing severe problems. As cities grew, tenements were built to house more people. Families were crowded into these foul-smelling, gloomy buildings. Diseases thrived in this unhealthy environment. Typhoid fever, scarlet fever, smallpox, and diphtheria became problems. Cities finally

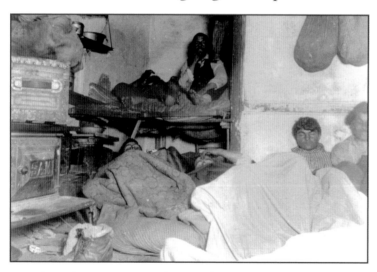

Immigrants crowd together in a tenement.

began to provide better sanitation services, such as better sewage disposal and garbage collection.

This picture from Harper's Weekly *illustrates
the poor conditions of tenement living.*

ROBBER BARONS AND STRIKERS

At this time, an element emerged to spur U.S. business. Giant corporations began to dominate several industries. These corporations were large companies in which people could invest their money. This accumulation of wealth permitted corporations to build extensive railroad lines and to fund other ambitious projects.

One of the most dominant corporations of the time was the Standard Oil Company. This company was founded by John D. Rockefeller, who had entered the oil business during the Civil War. In 1863, he built an oil refinery in Cleveland, Ohio. The refineries were needed to convert oil into kerosene, which was burned in lamps.

Rockefeller owned the country's largest refinery, but he strove to become even bigger in the oil

John D. Rockefeller

THE GILDED AGE

It was Mark Twain who invented the name "Gilded Age." The years following the Civil War were marked with political and corporate corruption. In one of the first political protest novels ever written in the United States, Twain mocked government politics. Many of the characters in the book are thinly disguised politicians and industrialists of the day. This book was entitled The Gilded Age.

This name was soon given to the era following the Civil War. People became obsessed with possessions, progress, and making money. Many people began to suffer to benefit a few who wanted to get rich quickly.

Mark Twain

For example, the U.S. government gave miles of land to railroads that laid new line in the west. These railroads, in turn, sold the land to settlers. The railroads then charged them a great deal of money to ship products by train to or from the settlers. The Gilded Age ended between the late 1800s and early 1900s with the coming of the Spanish-American War.

industry. He expanded his business by eliminating competitors. At first, Rockefeller bought rival companies. But his company also cut prices so low for kerosene that other oil companies could not compete.

Rockefeller's tactics were so successful that the Standard Oil Company eventually had a virtual monopoly in the oil industry. The methods used by the Standard Oil Company are known as horizontal integration. This meant reducing competition until a monopoly had been achieved in a market.

An ad for the Standard Oil Company   *Andrew Carnegie*

Another leading industrialist was Andrew Carnegie. He was a
Scottish immigrant who established an immense steel company.
Carnegie used vertical integration to build up his steel operation.

Vertical integration meant that Carnegie controlled all the steps to
produce and distribute his product. He owned mines in Minnesota
that supplied his steel mills in Pittsburgh with iron. Carnegie also
owned the railroads that transported his steel to market. In addition,
Carnegie's railroads created demand for the steel being churned out of
his mills.

Carnegie, Rockefeller, and other industrial leaders became very
wealthy from their enterprises. Many people condemned the way
these men conducted business. Some critics began to use the term
"robber baron" to describe America's chief industrialists. Those who

used this term believed businessmen used unfair methods to gain near monopolies. Critics also pointed out that business leaders became rich while many U.S. workers struggled to make a living.

Conflicts between workers and company owners became more hostile in the latter part of the nineteenth century. The number of strikes increased as workers demanded better pay and fewer hours. Strikes also became more violent.

A strike against the Baltimore & Ohio Railroad was brutal. In July 1877, the strike started in West Virginia and spread to other parts of the country. Violence broke out in several cities, including Baltimore, Maryland, and Chicago, Illinois. In Baltimore and Chicago, federal troops were called in to restore order. The strike ended in early August. By this time, millions of dollars in railroad property had been destroyed. Fighting had also killed about 50 people and injured hundreds of others.

Chicago was the scene of another violent event in the country's labor struggle in 1886. Workers around the country had been demanding an 8-hour workday. At the time, a normal workday was 12 hours. In Chicago, supporters of the 8-hour workday and striking manufacturing workers held a rally on May 3. Police broke up the demonstration, killing four protesters.

The next night, hundreds of people gathered in Chicago's Haymarket Square to protest the killings. Again, police arrived to disperse the crowd. This time an unknown person tossed a bomb among the police, killing eight of them. The police fired into the crowd. Another seven or eight people were killed and dozens were wounded, including police officers.

The incident became known as the Haymarket Square Riot. Police arrested eight anarchist leaders in connection with the violence. The anarchists believed that government authority was harmful. They carried out assassinations for their cause. No one knew who threw the bomb in Haymarket Square, but the arrests and later convictions damaged the labor movement. Some people began to connect labor leaders with anarchism.

In 1887, four of those convicted were hanged. One suspect committed suicide in jail. In 1893, Illinois governor John Peter Altgeld pardoned the other three prisoners. Altgeld studied the Haymarket Square Riot and believed the suspects had not received fair trials.

The violence of the labor movement was one example of the turmoil during the Industrial Revolution. These were times of broad change that produced both good and bad effects. Prices of goods fell and incomes rose. But the gap between the richest and poorest Americans widened. In 1890, the wealthiest 1 percent of Americans owned 51 percent of the property. The poorest 44 percent had only 1.2 percent.

Americans with good incomes had more choices than ever. They found they had more leisure time, and they began to spend money on entertainment. Americans began to watch organized sports and to attend circuses, theaters, and musicals.

Another change took place for Americans with extra money. They could spend their money on ready-made clothes and recent inventions such as the telephone. Large industries such as railroads, steel, and textiles still dominated the U.S. economy in 1900. But an economy based on consumer goods for the household was beginning to emerge.

The ability to produce an abundance of goods was an important result of the Industrial Revolution. This capability allowed industrial countries to support their growing populations. The United States, however, did more than simply provide enough for its people to survive. Americans overall experienced a better standard of living than people in other countries.

By 1900, the United States had surpassed Britain as the world's greatest industrial power. In fact, the nation produced more goods than Britain, France, and Germany combined. This productivity helped make the United States the richest country in the world. Within a century, the United States had gone from a country of farms and small towns to a nation of factories and flourishing cities. The changes the country had undergone were truly revolutionary.

A family sits down to a meal in the early twentieth century. They are surrounded by many consumer goods made in factories.

TIMELINE

1733 — John Kay receives a patent for the flying shuttle.

1768 — James Hargreaves invents the spinning jenny.

1769 — James Watt is granted a patent for his improvements to the steam engine.

Sir Richard Arkwright invents the water frame.

1790 — Samuel Slater establishes a cotton mill in Rhode Island. The mill is the first in the United States to use British technology in the textile industry.

1793 — Eli Whitney improves the cotton gin, which creates a boon for the cotton industry in the United States.

1807 — In August, Robert Fulton's steamboat the *Clermont* begins a successful voyage up the Hudson River.

1825 — The Erie Canal is completed in New York state. The canal links Buffalo to Albany, and allows New York City to receive goods from the west.

On September 27, George Stephenson operates a locomotive on the first railway.

1829 On August 8, the Stourbridge Lion becomes the first locomotive to operate on an American rail line.

1861 to 1865 The Civil War is fought between Northern and Southern states. The superior production capacity of the North helps it defeat the South.

1863 John D. Rockefeller builds his first oil refinery in Cleveland, Ohio. Rockefeller's business, the Standard Oil Company, later gains a near monopoly in the oil industry.

1877 In July, a strike against the Baltimore & Ohio Railroad becomes violent, leading to several deaths.

1886 On May 4, the Haymarket Square Riot occurs in Chicago, Illinois. Several police officers are killed by a bomb and many protesters are wounded.

1900 The United States is the wealthiest country in the world and the greatest industrial power.

American Moments

FAST FACTS

In the 1760s, Sir Richard Arkwright's efforts to build a water frame alarmed his neighbors. Strange noises came from Arkwright's workshop and men frequently entered and left the building. Neighbors were convinced the men were practicing witchcraft.

Steamboats improved transportation on the Mississippi River. But steamboats could also be dangerous. About 4,000 people died in steamboat disasters between 1810 and 1850. The worst U.S. disaster on a single ship happened on April 27, 1865. The boiler on the steamboat *Sultana* exploded, which led to about 1,700 deaths.

Labor strikes were common events in the late nineteenth century. Between 1881 and 1900, about 23,000 strikes occurred in the United States.

Many of the industrialists had reputations as robber barons. But some of them also gave millions of dollars to charities, universities, and other causes. For example, John D. Rockefeller donated $500 million during his lifetime. Andrew Carnegie distributed $350 million. Some of Carnegie's donations helped build 2,800 public libraries.

Between 1860 and 1900, the number of U.S. industrial workers increased from 1.3 million to 5.3 million.

WEB SITES
WWW.ABDOPUB.COM

Would you like to learn more about the Industrial Revolution? Please visit **www.abdopub.com** to find up-to-date Web site links about the Industrial Revolution and other American moments. These links are routinely monitored and updated to provide the most current information available.

A railroad train passes by the blast furnaces of the Carnegie Steel Corporation.

GLOSSARY

anarchism: a political belief that modern forms of government are harmful. Anarchism contends that society should be based on voluntary cooperation.

assassinate: to murder an important person.

black lung disease: a breathing disorder caused by inhaling coal dust.

civil war: a war between groups of the same country. The United States of America (Northern states) and Confederate States of America (Southern states) fought a civil war from 1861 to 1865.

colliery: a coal mine and its buildings.

crop rotation: the practice of alternately growing different crops on the same land.

diphtheria: a disease that affects the throat and can cause death.

kerosene: a petroleum product originally used to burn in lamps.

loom: a frame used to weave cloth.

monopoly: the complete control of a product, service, or industry.

pardon: to forgive anything illegal that a person has done.

refinery: the building and machinery for purifying petroleum.

Royal Society for the encouragement of Arts, Manufactures and Commerce:
an organization founded in Britain in 1754. The group's original aim
was to promote the development of a prosperous society.

scarlet fever: a disease caused by bacteria. The illness produces a red rash
and causes inflammation of the nose, throat, and mouth.

secede: to break away from a group.

smallpox: a disease that causes a blister-like rash, vomiting, fever, and
fatigue. The blisters become scars.

strike: a situation in which employees refuse to work. Employees usually
go on strike to put pressure on employers to offer higher wages or
better working conditions.

technology: the use of scientific knowledge to solve practical problems.

textile: of or having to do with designing, manufacturing, or producing
woven fabric.

tram: a cart that runs on rails in a mine.

typhoid fever: typhoid fever is a bacterial disease spread by lice that causes
fever and a dark red rash.

INDEX